*The Beginner's Book of*
# WATERCOLOUR PAINTING

PRUSSIAN BLUE    COBALT BLUE    LEMON CHROME    YELLOW OCHRE

MAKING A COLOUR CHART
*with two yellows (Lemon Chrome and Yellow Ochre)
and two blues (Prussian and Cobalt)*

*The Beginner's Book of*

# WATERCOLOUR PAINTING

---

written and illustrated by

## ADRIAN HILL

P.P.R.O.I., R.B.A.

BLANDFORD PRESS

POOLE   NEW YORK   SYDNEY

Blandford Press

an imprint of
Cassell plc
Artillery House, Artillery Row
London SW1P 1RT

First published 1959
Reprinted 1960,
1963, 1965, 1968, 1971,
1975, 1978
Reprinted in this paperback edition 1986
Reprinted 1987, 1989

ISBN 0 7137 1742 4

Distributed in the United States by
Sterling Publishing Co., Inc.,
2 Park Avenue, New York, NY 10016

Distributed in Australia by
Capricorn Link (Australia) Pty Ltd
PO Box 665, Lane Cove, NSW 2066

Printed in Great Britain by
Butler & Tanner Ltd, Frome and London

# Contents

For
SUSAN MARY PARRY

# Introduction

IN presenting this little book to the beginner, dare I state that, in contrast to the technique of oils, the medium of water-colour painting is not all that easy! I feel I must begin with this warning, because it is only too true and it would be unfair to imply otherwise. Indeed it would be folly, because I know from personal experience that to master this particular technique takes pluck, patience and pertinacity. But--and this is the great point— of all mediums to attempt, I still believe that water-colour is the most rewarding, as it always has been and always will be, a popular medium for English-speaking countries. And if this smacks of smugness, surely it is true to say that "we" have always excelled, in this form of expression, and it is high time this fact was reaffirmed.

I suppose it was in the first half of the nineteenth century that the art of water-colour painting reached its zenith, and the acknowledged head of the English school was J. M. W. Turner. No book on this medium can neglect paying tribute to his genius, for while the best of his contemporaries is outstanding for one or two special beauties of manner and effect, Turner is remarkable for all. "He was not only technically the equal, if not the master, but he comprehended them without exception."

Today we can still turn to his works in this field for inspiration, for apart from their technical skill, there is always their individuality which marks them out among the work of all other water-colourists, however great.

With such notable examples, why, I wonder, is water-colour

painting in danger of being played down or made to appear so easy? Of course you can "have fun" with water-colours (indeed I hope I shall be able to prove this), but it is *serious* fun and does connote a real measure of study. We have only to thumb the how-to-do-it books and glance at their titles to sense how anxious are the artist-writers to beguile the reader with the belief that success will come without undue strain on hand, eye or mind. And as I know only too well how rightly incensed the serious reader is when he realises that he has been "led up the garden", I shall make no bones about it but repeat that water-colour painting is no easy matter, and it wouldn't be such a truly lovely form of expression if it were!

Having said that, I can immediately comfort and encourage the beginner by the assurance that if such advice as I can give is properly understood, digested and put into practice, there are no limits to the *personal* way in which this technique can be pursued with increasing enjoyment. Once—and I must re-emphasise this—once the foundations have been truly and firmly laid.

What you do with the medium, when once you know how to handle it, is no affair of mine. You can stick to the traditional way of painting or strike out for a personal technique. All I can hope to do is to excite your desire to learn the ropes and then have the courage to break out in all directions!

And to the general reader I would hasten to add that the best way in which he may hope to benefit from his reading is to select just that piece of instructional advice which is apposite to his immediate purpose.

# CHAPTER ONE

# Materials

FIRST, the tools of the trade. Colours come first. Now every professional water-colour painter I know has very definite and different views about what colours to use and what to avoid. This is inevitable—one man's meat . . . One will favour a certain blue, or yellow, another will swear by a particular red, while a third abjures any made-up green. The right choice must in the end be a personal choice, the outcome of experience and practice—a matter of trial and error.

If I suggest the following list, it is because it is what I would call a safe palette, to which you can add from time to time especially when your subject-matter demands a local colour you do not possess.

Three yellows—Lemon chrome, Yellow ochre, Raw sienna.
Three reds—Alizarin crimson, Light red, Vermilion.
Three blues—Prussian, Cobalt, Ultramarine.
Two browns—Burnt sienna, Vandyke brown.
One green—Viridian.
One black—Ivory.

If you think thirteen is an unlucky number I suggest you omit Raw sienna, or Ultramarine! Cerulean blue, Paynes grey, Raw umber and Brown madder are all useful but in no way indispensable.

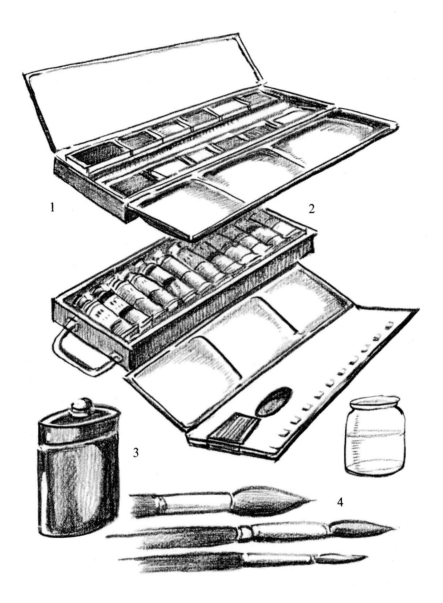

1 Half or whole pan box (*japanned tin*) for *12* colours
2 Whole tube box for *12* colours, with handle, and with palette
 as detachable lid of box
3 Water container with detachable dipper for outdoor sketching
4 Brushes—sable or squirrel hair. Large, medium and small
5 Jam-jar, as water container, for painting indoors

There are, on the other hand, certain colours which, if I list them here, I do so as a warning and not as a veto. I would look askance at Antwerp blue, Bistre, Brown pink, Orange cadmium, Emerald green, Gamboge, Green bice, Indigo, Hooker's green, Mars brown, Mauve, Naples yellow, Sap green and Neutral tint. I should call them "fancy goods". It is very easy to be led astray by their attractive names, but whether you buy the lot and weed out, or begin with a few and build up, must be left to your discretion.

*Paper.* A good make of thick drawing paper either purchased by the sheet, cut to the required size and pinned to your drawing-board, or bought in pad form of a serviceable size (not less than 15 in. by 11 in.), is entirely dependable, takes the colours well, and is especially economical for studies and "try-outs".

Water-colour paper can be obtained in many makes, weights and textures, again in sheets or made up in pads.

Finally there are pasteless boards, which are, I find, ideal for bold outdoor work. They can be obtained in various weights, do not need stretching and, may I add, can be painted on both sides!

Hot pressed paper is too smooth for general work, but can be recommended for delicate flower paintings, or any subject that demands a high finish. It is especially good for reproduction.

*Brushes.* Sables, which are by far the best and have the longest life, are expensive. Squirrel, on the other hand, have not the same pliant quality, nor the life, but can be recommended to start off with and are a reasonable price. For the beginner, only three sizes of brush are necessary: a big broad one (10 or 11) for large washes; a medium (7–8) for drawing the forms; and a fine one (3–4) for detail work. These should be kept scrupulously clean and fashioned into a point when dried.

There are on the market a number of water-colour boxes already filled with colours, but it is far wiser to buy an empty box and fill it with the colours I have mentioned. I have drawn examples of the boxes which I use myself, and you will see that one has little slots in one lid for squeezing colours from the tube, and three deep sections in the opposite lid for colour mixing. The pans, if pans you buy, can when empty be refilled with fresh colour from tubes, and the box should be long enough to keep your brushes in. A flat, japanned bottle with a screw lid for your water, and some soft rag, or sponge, and your equipment is complete.

As in oil painting, if you are working out of doors you will need a sketching stool, but an easel is not absolutely necessary as you can nurse your block on your knee and hold your box by the ring at the base, on your thumb, while painting.

# CHAPTER TWO

# Colour Chart

IN my experience, greens and greys are the chief stumbling-blocks in colour mixing for the beginner. As in the medium of oil painting, I consider the making of a colour chart to be of inestimable value, for only by this methodical means will the student be made aware what surprising variations in tint and tone can be obtained by the judicious blending of a few basic colours. With two blues and two yellows, for instance, practically all the different tints of green in Nature can be matched. This will be seen from the colour chart opposite the title page.

The initial colours must be painted in at full strength, as it will be by the added increase of water that the mixtures will become lighter and more transparent in texture. Moreover, by adding more of one colour to the other, the result will become either colder (bluer) or warmer (richer in yellow) in tint, as the case may be.

A rewarding range of greens can be obtained by ringing the changes on either of these blue and yellow combinations: Prussian blue with Yellow ochre and then with Lemon chrome; Cobalt blue with Yellow ochre and then with Lemon chrome. And all these resultant greens can be obtained without using your Viridian! Incidentally, this made-up green mixed with either of the above-mentioned yellows will produce yet another range of cool or warm tints. (On its own, Viridian is far too cold for any

Nature green, but as I have indicated above is a useful adjunct in such colour blendings.)

With greys, you can experiment to your heart's content! Try out for yourself such combinations as: Cobalt or Cerulean blue with Light red or Vermilion; Prussian blue with Burnt sienna; Cobalt blue with Vandyke brown; Viridian with Light red; Ivory black with Prussian or Cobalt blue. Ample water is required to dilute these pigments while results can be further muted—or neutralised—by a touch of Yellow ochre or Black. For it must be remembered that all greys in Nature have a bias towards some colour—such as a yellowish grey, bluish grey, greenish grey, pinkish grey. Without this colour tendency our greys would be lifeless and could be achieved merely by diluting Ivory black.

These manifold shades of grey should not be taken for granted but put into practice, for it is only when you have *seen* for *yourself*, either by imitation, emulation or experiment, that your knowledge of colour mixing will develop and your consequent range of tints increase under your control and authority.

I should add that Chinese white can be mixed with all water-colours, and what is lost in transparency is often made up for in something more third-dimensional in form, especially in architectural subjects, where solidity in surface can achieve what I can only call fabric substance. Again, experiment alone will demonstrate its advantages and perhaps its attendant snags!

I have purposely refrained in this chapter from using a colour reproduction of my own grey chart for two reasons. One is that, however well intentioned the colour block maker is, unless many printings are used, the results are more an approximation of the colours than a true version of them. When demonstrating such subtle variations as are implied in my instructions, anything short of perfection in truth of actual shade is both frustrating to the author and confusing and misleading to the reader.

The other and more cogent reason is that I want you to *make* a chart of your *own* and not use one *ready made* for you! In the other colour reproduction, the near miss—if I may so term it—does not matter so much as it is primarily the general colour effect that is aimed for, and which, despite reproduction, is successfully achieved.

· In this matter of preferences and prejudices with reference to colour mixtures, especially that of green, it is of interest to note that with some professional water-colourists, more than two colours are used to make the required shade. In particular, may I quote one of them: "I mixed a full strong wash of green (burnt sienna, monastral blue, cobalt blue, rose madder, oxide of chromium, raw sienna and cerulean—varying the wash by using more or less of these colours)." No less than seven, you see, are brought into action. This may appear to the reader as rather excessive, but it might be well worth while following the prescription in order to see whether the result does agree with your idea of what "a full strong green" should be!

The point I wish to stress is that in technique, in which mixing is a part, there are and should be many alternative routes to the desired goal, for it is this freedom that ensures the fulfilment of a personal way of painting.

# CHAPTER THREE

# *Washes*

ONE of the indispensable prerequisites for a successful
water-colour painting is to be able to lay even and
graduated washes of one or more colours. This is far easier than
it sounds. All that is needed is a sufficient quantity of the required
colour or colours already mixed, a large brush, fully charged, and
a steady hand. Have your paper at a slight slant—a thickish book
underneath your drawing-board will give it the required tilt.
Then carry your brushful of colour *lightly* and evenly across the
top of your drawing—if you are right-handed—from the left-
hand side. The weight of colour will descend to the base of the
line as your paper is at a slight angle, and this you will catch up
with your next wash, having recharged your brush and again
proceeding in the same direction. Do not work backwards as the
movement won't be so steady. There is no hurry; the more
deliberate the operation, the more evenly the washes will dry.
When you reach the last line of colour the surplus moisture can
be absorbed by carrying a clean, dry brush lightly and slowly
across.

After a little practice, you can tint a sheet in any colour with
an even finish up to 22 in. by 15 in. with perfect ease. But you
must have plenty of colour to cover the desired area.

The next step is to graduate your colour from its full strength
to its palest tint. This is accomplished by adding water to
your brush after each succeeding line of wash. As you proceed

downwards you will replenish your brush with less and less of the colour and more from the water container, until you are only dipping your brush into and using the water for your wash.

Prussian or Cobalt blue are excellent colours for such exercises as the result of the graduated wash contains the principle of all clear sky paintings in that the positive blue at the top will decrease in strength (as it does in Nature) until only the faintest blush of blue is visible directly over the horizon, thus giving the dome-like structure of the heavens.

Now you can experiment with blending of one colour into another. Have the second tint mixed and introduce it when the first colour is at half strength, about half-way down. Again, do not become flustered and begin dragging your brush backwards and forwards—or worse still, up and down! From blue to blue-green, then to a greeny yellow and even to a touch of red at the bottom, and you have incidentally proved to yourself that cool colours "go back" and that warm colours "come forward"; and this will help you a lot when it comes to selecting the right tint for such passages as need recession or projection.

As I have written elsewhere, the student should, even at this early stage, be free to conduct further exercises in his own way and investigate the possibilities of as many combinations and blendings as he feels will be of benefit to a more complete under-standing of his craft. Damping the paper first, for example, before laying the above-mentioned washes, not forgetting that the colour will be weakened by being laid on a moist surface; superimposing one wash on another, remembering in this case to see that the first wash is dry before the second is applied.

In short, the less drudgery that is indicated in such practices, the more the student will be encouraged to make his own inquiries. Nevertheless, I would venture to add one or two warnings. Change your water fairly frequently: discoloured water, after a time, will affect your colour washes, diminishing their pristine transparency. Be careful to cleanse your brushes thoroughly, especially those you have used with a strong colour like Prussian blue or Alizarin crimson. If you are working with pans of colour, the same care should be taken to remove any trace of another tint which may remain to discolour the surface of the pan, especially if it happens to be any hint of green, say on a yellow or a red. After use, all the surfaces of the different pans of colour should be moistened with clean water to remove any stain of another pigment: and the same applies to the receptacles or trays in which the colour washes have left stains of drying colour. Unexpected discoloration can be caused to a fresh wash unless all traces of previous colour are removed with water and a clean rag.

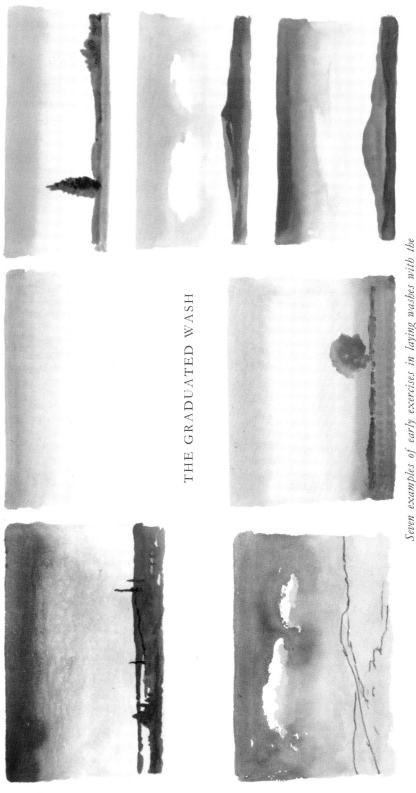

## THE GRADUATED WASH

*Seven examples of early exercises in laying washes with the
introduction of clouds and silhouettes of trees and distant horizons*

# CHAPTER FOUR

# Still Life Exercise

IN order to practise the technique and master the correct matching of tint and tone, there is much to be said for painting an arrangement of a few simple objects. Bottles are excellent for this exercise, for they have the merit of remaining static for as long a period as it takes to paint them; and in the early stages I need hardly add it is a great comfort to know that your properties won't "die on you". Moreover, bottles, transparent and of different colours, make straightforward models; their various shapes are basically uniform, their high lights precise, revealing the contours and incidentally giving to the surface its glassy quality. It is therefore very important to note exactly *where* these high lights occur and, if possible, to leave their little shapes uncovered by your washes of local colour. They can, of course, be retrieved by "lifting" with a small, stiffish brush or by the point of a penknife or Chinese white, but the undisturbed whiteness of the paper gives the best results.

When you have lightly indicated the shapes of your group you should dispense with your pencil and rely on your brush to confirm their individuality, match their colour and render them solid.

If your background is lighter in tone than that of the bottles (and this I advise for a first exercise), a wash of this colour at full strength can be passed over your *whole* drawing (except the high lights), and while waiting for this to dry, mix up a middle tint of the local colour of each bottle, that is, the shade *next* in *tone* to the high light. This wash can be laid *all over* each form, skirting round the high lights. Then the next wash in order of tone will be applied where it occurs and finally the darkest colour on the shadow side will be painted in. In short, you will be painting from light to dark. (See A and C, page 22.)

As a corrective to having to paint more than one wash for each stage, it is a good plan to test out their strength by mixing the tint on a separate piece of paper, remembering that every colour wash will be shades lighter when it dries out. If these washes in turn can be applied before the preceding one is *quite dry*, the right merging will give the roundness to the form and prevent edgeness. I don't say this is easy, but with practice you will be surprised to find how well the colours will behave, if you don't chivvy them about! Excessive concern for tidiness should play no part in the performance. Indeed, even in such a deliberate exercise as this, a certain looseness of handling is recommended in order to obviate too many signs of labour.

I don't pretend that the result (illustration (C)) is anything but a tight conscientous study, but I do maintain that what has been learnt from such sustained concentration on the facts will stand you in good stead when it comes to attempting a freer translation, an example of which is hopefully submitted in illustration (B). For having schooled yourself to paint a literal statement, you will have more confidence to loosen up and take artistic liberties with both the matter of your subject—I chose another bottle and added some fruit—and your manner of describing it.

For you should now try and dispense with any preliminary drawing and start in right away with the brush and with plenty of colour, and let nothing hold up operations such as coaxing little blobs of colour to stay put, or attempting to rectify a ragged

*A Stages one and two*

*B Freedom of handling*

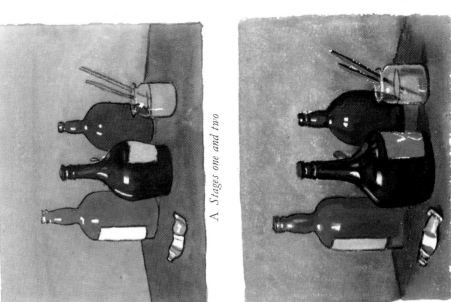

*C Final stage*

*D Drawing direct with the brush*

contour or repainting a lost outline. Only by such legitimate freedom of execution will you be able in the end to justify snappng your fingers at discretion and the chains of a conventional technique. I should add that to assist further with your aim for a spontaneous impression, you should damp the surface of your paper first. This will necessitate accelerating the tempo of the painting and prevent what has been so aptly described as "caressing each object separately". In short, from start to finish, a sense of urgency—I can think of no better word—should dominate the performance, and the natural exhaustion from such a concentrated effort will be matched by a sense of satisfaction unknown to the plodding but pusillanimous practitioner with the brush.

From inanimate objects the student can attempt simple flower arrangements, like that in illustration (D). In the end all the drawing of the individual blooms and leaves can be accomplished with the brush and on a surface which has been first damped with a sponge. And remember, it is always better to aim at an *impression* of flowers rather than produce them laboriously as single botanical specimens, each with a label!

I think I should add that if such faithful representation is desired, then a *portrait* of the flower should be first drawn in, say on tinted paper, and heightened with discreet washes of colour to which Chinese white can be legitimately introduced with charming results.

# CHAPTER FIVE

# *Composition*

NO instructional book on any medium can exclude a chapter on Composition. If the reader thinks he knows all the rules, he can skip this one, but the beginner would be unwise if he thinks he is fully knowledgeable of all that is implied by a proper arrangement of his subject-matter. Because that is what composition is all about, and to be forewarned is of more practical value than having to bow to the wiser head and admit the truth of the gentle admonishment, "I told you so!"

What are these warnings, these "told you so's"? I would say the most important is: "Are you completely satisfied that you have chosen the best view-point for your painting, and if so, just how much are you going to include of the view and how much are you going to leave out?" The next question would be: "Has your subject got an eye, a focal point of interest, and where is it to be placed?" Not, it is hoped, right in the middle or close to the side of your picture. Then, what about your foreground? Have you allowed a sufficient interval between the bottom of your picture and your foreground objects—tree, barn, haystack, fence, whatever they may be? Foregrounds can be the very devil—any professional painter will tell you this much! They must occupy only as much depth and contain only as much detail interest as the eye can "sense" rather than wish to contemplate, for this area is a sort of "jumping off" ground for the eye to travel into the middle distance, a subtle but secure platform from

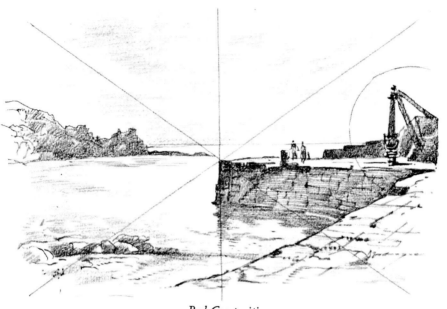

*Bad Composition*

*Same view with improved placing of the various forms without sacrificing its topographical features*

*How much the eye can comfortably take in without
redrawing the scene*

which the beholder will view your picture at ease. It must therefore satisfy but not excite too much interest in itself.

Then, again, are some of your shapes—for the intervals
*between* solid forms become shapes—too wide or too regular, and
are they pleasant in outline? You see there are a lot of *little*
things, but all very important, if your composition is to be
acceptable, all over.

I have often been at pains to explain with regard to these
questions that rarely, if ever, does Nature offer you a ready-
made "off the peg" subject that does not need alterations before
it can be said to "fit" pictorially. And I am always presenting
this self-imposed responsibility, not as an irksome task, but as a
privilege which the photographer cannot enjoy. For however
much care be taken to find the ideal subject and the best position

OPPOSITE

TOP—*The view as it appeared in Nature*.

BOTTOM—*The same view where the rules of composition have
necessitated minor readjustments so that the eye can travel over the
bridge and into the picture, and not across it*

to photograph it from, the scene must then be reproduced exactly as it *happens to appear* in Nature. The photographer, as far as I know, can alter nothing, add nothing, nor leave out anything. In short, he cannot really be said to impose his personality on the view. And it is just here that the artist scores. He can! Slight as the modifications may be, they can make all the difference between—well—the ordinary and the extra-ordinary. If this were not so, with the continual improvement of colour photography and in the ability of the camera to "freeze a moment in time", the landscape painter would be outdistanced and outclassed in all his outdoor painting and would be well advised to turn his attention to non-figurative abstractions.

Indeed, there is a growing tendency to turn the back on Nature, for, I believe, this very reason. But it is only a fallacy, for I am convinced that there is still a wealth of unexplored subject-matter in Nature if only we know how to use our eyes and fashion our will to succeed. Composition, then, is *one* of the keys which can unlock the door which so often bars the way to our desire to contribute something sincerely felt and personally experienced amidst all the challenging aspects of this countryside of ours.

In the illustrations I have tried to give examples of some of these compositional problems, and to show where they are to be met with and the various ways of sorting them out.

FIGURES IN LANDSCAPES (OPPOSITE)

TOP—*The small figurehead on the left of the door of the inn is sufficient in itself, but the human figure by the far doorway is introduced to carry the eye from the centre of the sketch*

BOTTOM—*The figures were drawn in to add life without movement and "dress" the scene*

*A good example of "overdressing" the scene with too many figures*

*Without the two figures and the chickens, the foreground would have been very empty*

# CHAPTER SIX

# Stages in Water-colour Painting

THE ideal technique is, of course, the direct one, in which you finish as you go, the stages melting into each other without pause for waiting for this or that to dry. I know it sounds quite out of reach to the beginner but it's the one to aim for. Even in the early days, I do not favour overmuch the "safety first" slogan (that sombre warning about learning to walk before you try to run), and rather plead instead the limiting of the number of stages so that the performance runs smoothly and does not disclose a jerky technique. A good drawing (as I will keep repeating) is essential before you begin the actual painting. Then, if your subject is a landscape with a fair proportion of sky, the first question to be answered is: "Does one paint the sky first and then work down from the horizon to the foreground, or leave the sky area till last?"

I think this query can be settled in two ways. If what is happening in the sky (by which I mean a definite cloud effect) is of major importance to the pictorial effect of your subject, and if your landscape should happen to be a low horizon view, as it may well be, then you should certainly paint that area first, boldly and swiftly, because it must affect the colours of the landscape beneath; and once you've established the pervading mood, you will see more clearly how the tone and colour of Nature's forms will be influenced and paint them in accordingly. If, on the other hand, you have chosen a high horizon, then you

FIRST STAGE *The subject having been firmly drawn in, the sky, which is of major importance, is painted in first*

SECOND STAGE *The sky having been washed in, the shadow sides of the various river craft are painted in to fix where the light is coming from*

THIRD STAGE *The sky and the landscape having been coloured, the figures are painted in at full strength, to emphasise their pictorial importance*

FOURTH STAGE *As seven-eighths of the picture in this case is occupied with Nature's forms, the sky was painted in at this stage, the wash of pale blue being taken over the trees, leaving only the last touches in the landscape to be added,* if and where necessary would be well advised to leave that sky portion till last. You will then see better what sort of a sky is required. Also, to have a strip of white paper left at the top of your painting will ensure that you keep the pitch of your landscape high in tone and when you do paint the sky you will know exactly what is required in colour, design (if any) and tone. That I would say is logical in both cases.

I have said *"when* you do paint the sky", and I am reminded of a water-colour painter of some repute whom I knew who never painted in the sky at the actual time of working on the spot, but introduced what he thought suitable for the subject days and sometimes weeks afterwards, in the security of his studio; and passed this on as a safe tip. The result to me always looked artificially conceived, skilful as his skies always were: they were never, if I may express it so, happily wedded to the view underneath. To my mind, therefore, whenever the sky is painted it should be done at the time of the actual performance.

Another reason for painting the sky in first is that while in oils you paint from dark to light (superimposing your lights on your darks), in water-colours you must necessarily reverse the axiom and paint from light (for the sky is, after all, the origin of light) to dark, because in principle all Nature's forms *receive* light but do not *give* it, and must be, except in certain climatic conditions, lower in key than the tones of the sky above. And in both cases your white paper must be retained for your highest light.

Stages do occur, however, when for instance, you arrive at those areas in your landscape where it is advisable to float on a wash, say, of Yellow ochre as a ground tint for a subsequent wash of more positive or local colour. I am thinking primarily in the matter of greens, which to the beginner are generally seen as too cold a colour, especially for trees and meadows in the early spring. This preliminary wash of yellow will warm up these passages. Other stages or pauses will happen towards the end of your painting, when it may be necessary to accentuate—or modify—an accent, more generally to degrade some harsh or strident colour which may now be seen to be out of harmony with the desired colour scheme.

But apart from these natural deliberations, I can think of nothing so laborious as painting with one eye on your subject and one on some instructional book, where rules of procedure are sacrosanct. In passing, I remember one textbook in my youth which insisted on several distinct intervals in the performance when a wash of pure water floated over the entire work was enforced, "to soften edges and bring the painting together!" All that this expedient accomplished in my case was to turn my paper into a series of hurried wet undulations and any desire on my part to proceed was effectually "washed out"!

The life of the work must be preserved at all costs, but such aids as the above, like artificial respiration do not bear contemplating! There are washes *and* washes and the only kind that are wanted, I have already described.

BRIXHAM HARBOUR

WALBERSWICK                    (*By permission of G. B. Coleman, Esq.*)

REFLECTIONS OF BOATS: CORNWALL

CHAPTER SEVEN

# Subject-matter

I SUPPOSE one could say that almost any subject can be painted in water-colours, so long as it can be visualised clearly in the terms of the medium. In other words, a subject that you can execute within the scope and time of the technique, swift and sure in handling and free from any sign of labour. The reader will learn by experience to sense that rightness, expressed in the spontaneous ejaculation, "There's a good subject for a water-colour", against the dubious speculation, "The subject is fine but will it make a water-colour?" It is that question "Will it make . . ." that should rule it out, because it implies an uncertainty as to one's capabilities of seeing it through in one sitting. It suggests some problem that might necessitate the repainting of a particular part to make a more satisfactory rendering possible, which inevitably occurs when a painting is built up in more than one sitting.

Now with a pure water-colour (in my opinion) no repainting is really possible, no attempted rescue operations are entirely successful, and once your painting "springs a leak", it is far better to abandon the "sinking" picture and start another.

What sort of subject, then, is fool-proof for this medium?

Open, atmospheric landscapes, of course, but please not always low horizons and serene skies or still waters and a hazy distance! River and treescapes—rural scenes with farm buildings —street scenes—shipping—industry—architecture—interiors and figure subjects are all good grist to the painter's mill. Good drawing is essential in all of them especially those in which the human element is introduced, and absolutely indispensable if portraits are attempted; for to retain freshness of handling and the likeness of your sitter at the same time, an expert facility with the brush is required, which only years of patient practice can make perfect—and even then, the result has an unfortunate habit of looking old-fashioned. A tinted drawing (about which I shall say something later), if handled boldly, is more contemporary.

Flowers, by all means, for they can always make attractive and spirited water-colours. But here the danger of their looking old-fashioned lurks as much in the arrangement as in the handling, and the latter, if perfection in the botanical details of the flowers is insisted on, can rob the result of any progressive outlook. Certain it is that the typical "country bunch", if the container

OPPOSITE

TOP—*The mass of the trees and the distance having been indicated lightly, the sky is next painted boldly over the trees and a preliminary wash of warm colour is introduced for the foreground*

BOTTOM—*Now the trees can be painted at full strength over the sky, and finally the low horizon landscape can be finished with necessary detail in its local colour*

*An example of strong lighting to ensure architectural solidity and to emphasise pattern*

*An example of a small object (the farm shed) balancing the great tree on the right*

*Another example of a vertical (tree) and horizontal (ruin) form balancing each other*

*Vertical forms to counteract the steep perspective of the wall*

*Area in which the eye should come to rest*

*The danger of the tree following the sloping line of the old bridge*

*The arrows indicate how the eye should travel round the tree forms*

stands on a highly polished table on which a fallen bloom has been "tastefully" placed, will damn it at once in the eyes of the modern beholder. And quite right too! Stock flower compositions and sweet colour are two factors that have always bedevilled flower paintings in water-colours, and a glance round any amateur art exhibition will offer all the incriminating evidence required.

DRAWING

It has been said—I've said it myself on countless occasions—until it has become the archetype of all instructional precepts, that "painting is drawing with the brush". But however much this platitude is plugged, the warning is often ignored. In fact, the argument often appears to go like this: Painting is fun, therefore it must be easy. Drawing is a bore, therefore it must be difficult. So let's cut out the drawing and press on with the painting!

Now I will agree that with some kind of oil painting you can "get away with it", as we say, with the minimum of drawing (or hope you can, because the lack of it will surely find you out in the end), but in water-colours drawing is as essential as, well, rhythm is to dancing, for the reason that your brush must state and follow the form while it applies the colour, just as your feet subconsciously follow the tempo of the music and mark its character and form. Drawing and painting must keep in step.

A good working knowledge of drawing is therefore all-important because it will become increasingly obvious that the less laboured or corrected pencil construction there is to be seen under the washes of colour, the less laborious the finished effect. And in order to draw with authority and without repeated alterations, you should practise with the pencil on the spot and in the *same size* as you will paint. This needs diligence, as all extraneous detail must be eliminated and only those forms which you will be "clothing with colour" will be stated with sensitive precision. In particular, the guiding lines for any cloud formation must be only the faintest suggestion; in fact the actual drawing of individual cloud shapes should really be left to the brush, if anything like an atmospheric quality is to be preserved. This, I need hardly add, must be for some time a matter of trial and error. But if you can *draw*, then boldness, even to the point of recklessness—perhaps "chancing your arm" denotes less risk of foolhardiness—will achieve your aim, especially, and this I would plead with you, if you leave what you have painted and do not attempt to tidy it up or fuss it around. The more spontaneous the gestures and direction of your brush strokes, the more limpid or moving, in short more "sky like", your skies will be!

I do not care how well "designed" your sky may be, an overworked cloud effect will remain heavy in form and become turgid in colour; it won't go back, but will hover over your landscape with sinister solidity.

After all, vigour and breadth of treatment are synonymous with the boldness I have stated above, and these are qualities which can be ensured as long as the student takes care to retain his first impression of the scene—both in sky or landscape subject-matter—and to realise that the initial survey can never encompass a fraction of the elaborate detail which emerges when our eyes become accustomed to the scene. Above all, drawing, good drawing, breeds vigour and implements breadth of treatment.

HANDLING

Water-colour offers a pictorial medium that no other technical process can suitably replace. For its true expression it demands an inherent lightness of touch and in its pure form (as distinct from gouache) a transparency of wash.

*In the study of waves breaking on the rocks, a great deal depends on how much white paper is left uncovered. And in order to enhance the whiteness of the spray, the tone of the solid forms must be sufficiently lowered to achieve the violent impacts*

*In the study of the high seas, the brush must follow the rhythmic lines caused by the undulatory swell of the water*

*In the study of the river, all depends on the precise touch of the reflections, drawn in and left. In each case, no overpainting is possible if the wetness and movement of the water is to be preserved*

To the unimaginative student, the many ways of handling the medium, which could be more correctly described as "manu-facturing water-colours", depend solely on dexterity of execution, and this alone can only produce a meretricious picture which lacks the original integrity of the medium.

To the imaginative student, on the other hand, what his hand is taught to perform is determined by the mind, and thus the handling is free from affectation, and he can claim his right to sign it as his own. For it must never be forgotten that the indefinable touch of a master, although possessing the strongest stamp of character, is generally quite unfit to afford any practical information to a beginner and offers no practicable manner of imitation.

Indeed, handling must grow naturally and cannot be artificially forced. Our resolve must always be to look at Nature with an independent vision and with the desire to comprehend her in our own way, and not with any wish to see in her what others have discovered. And attempts to teach the representation of Nature by technical flourishes or indefinable symbols, possessing only a remote allusion to the intended subject, are of no practical use, as they furnish no clue or ground to proceed on towards the study of Nature or the mastery of the technique by which the knowledge is communicated. We must therefore return to the perception of the artist—to that urge from which springs the initiative in selecting his subject and the best personal means of conveying the effect. No technical embellishments, as I know from past experience, can ever atone for the lack of a personal composition, and no amount of finish can make repara-tion for flimsy fabric design. And in the last analysis, "finish", I would say, can only be satisfactorily answered according to the wish of each individual.

To free oneself of the chains which impede a spontaneous impression, any careful preliminary drawing must be abandoned. Whether working from imagination, as in the top illustration, or attempting a swift summary from life (still life interior in the case of the lower), a fully charged brush and plenty of colour, and a sense of urgency, are indispensable to success.

Squeeze out plenty of colour and have at least three brushes to hand and two containers of water, for, once started, nothing should hold up the performance.

You will see in the top example that the wash of Prussian blue with a touch of Black which I've used for the night sky has a granulated finish, due to the rough surface of the paper. The tiny particles of white paper where the colour has not "taken" are left, adding to, rather than detracting from, the haze or vibration of the artificial illumination of the scene. The eye of the top sketch is the floodlit building enhanced in drama by the hustle and bustle in the street beneath and flanked by the dark silhouette of the building on the left. A suggested lamp-standard was introduced to give proportional emphasis to the height of the central building.

In the bottom impression a corner of a bedroom is attempted. I first mixed up the tint for the wallpaper, introducing the pattern with quick, light touches while it was still damp. I left the shape of the picture empty until the end, because that was going to be the focal feature. The curtains, dressing table and other furniture were painted in boldly and left. No consideration for detail was allowed to slow up the performance.

OPPOSITE
TOP—*Unscripted impression*

BOTTOM—*Snapshot impression*

ROUND THE CLOCK

I have chosen a simple rock and sea composition (which I have varied slightly to obviate monotony), as seen under four different lightings, subject to the time of day. The illustrations suggest (they can do no more) how important a part lighting can play in altering the tonal composition of the scene and in helping the beginner to decide on the climatic conditions best suited to a subject.

The clear morning light often puts an edge on the forms; outlines are clear-cut and anything approaching a romantic rendering is sacrificed to a factual statement.

The light at noon generally affords more scope for variety in light and shade, softening the precise silhouette of the principal forms.

The afternoon light can cause gradual or sudden climatic changes which further alters the balance of light and shade, deepening the shadows and pin-pointing the high lights.

Under the direct top lighting of a moon, further tonal contrasts are introduced, which lend mystery to an otherwise conventional scene by spot-lighting the focal points of interest, thus helping to dramatise the subject-matter.

MORNING

NOON

AFTERNOON

MOONLIGHT

*Note local colour of tree trunks*

*Treatment of evening sky with distant trees*

# CHAPTER EIGHT

# *Approach*

A READINESS to adapt oneself to circumstances and try out any new method which appears most appropriate for the task upon which one is engaged is an important factor in the practice of water-colour, and as long as the experiments are conducted with intelligence they are calculated to safeguard the student against the charge of becoming stereotyped, a failing to which all artists are from time to time exposed. Especially is this regrettable if the student is content to copy an admired style rather than strive to develop a style of his own.

As this particular kind of modesty is almost an obsession with some amateurs, I make no excuse for repeating here that a personal rendering of Nature, however awkward or feeble it may appear, is much more worth while artistically than the best "copy" of the best style perfected by anybody else. This second-hand method of mastering the medium can so easily and subtly dictate the manner of all future productions, and this must inevitably put a brake on enterprise and invention. Indeed it is this insidious concern with the "know how" that has done such a disservice to the medium, and in so many cases has completely suffocated any desire for a personal statement. To be lured by technical virtuosity is to blind the eye to aesthetic defects which such paintings so often contain. In short, as somebody once said, admiring the polish and forgetting the table!

## SOME WARNINGS

I have said elsewhere, and I hope it is worth repeating here, that the authority which the teacher exercises when he pronounces some rigid dictum of technique is often found to conflict in a bewildering fashion with what is manifested in some of his own paintings! Moreover, the written word must not always be taken as gospel. For instance, the statement in a well-known treatise on water-colours which I thumbed recently that "Reflections should be *lighter* than the thing reflected" is obviously untrue. In fact it is the exact opposite—a white fence, for example, when reflected in water will be seen to be "off white", as water in bulk, that is, which has depth and a solid bottom, is never crystal clear and in consequence of this, and the natural discoloration, renders reflections of all solids a degree or two lower in tone. All the teacher can say with safety is that it may on occasions be found more "*pictorially*" correct to paint in the reflections lighter than they appear in Nature.

Just the same criticism can be levelled at the assertion that "water is a mirror reflecting light, and therefore, apart from any dark reflection which may occur, it will be as *light* as the *sky*." How can it be, if it only *receives* light? Once again, to state that "water is flat" (one knows what is meant) ignores all the circumstances when the surface is undulating or choppy or broken by waves—and, in fact, is anything but flat!

The point I wish to make is that dictums like the above can become formulas and woe betide the student who develops "a way" of painting—skies—or trees—or water—according to the book! A natural veneration that many beginners cultivate for the professional painter and all that he paints and *writes* can prove a heavy handicap to the development of the student's personality, as I know, for this slavish reverence has often led to a complete surrender of the student's urge to be himself.

Compare, by all means, one artist's style and approach with another's, and *judge for yourself* whether the execution adds or detracts from your pleasure when viewing the result as a whole.

On some occasions what the artist has "seen" in the subject may be far removed from what is actually there—and this should stimulate your desire to do likewise, for intricate detail can be suggested without burdening the subject with precise representation, and this should be remembered especially when attempting water and reflections!

EXPERIMENT

Once the fundamental rules of the technique have been accepted, the student should try out his own wings, experimenting being to my mind as important as experience! It will certainly prevent a pervading intention from degenerating into what can so easily become an inflexible convention—for if in everything one paints the predominant desire is to produce a water-colour which presents only the facts of Nature in an orderly arrangement, then such a mundane practice must surely deteriorate into a dull performance.

And while there must always be differences of opinion as to how far the medium can be exploited to secure the right personal expression or achieve the technical character which is aimed at, the accustomed approach often will be found unhelpful; and even if such experiments induce an attempt to be unconventional, I would never discourage this empirical approach, for it counts for something, if the desire to substitute for a dry formality a more personal mode of expression is adopted than that which is customary or in fashion at the moment. Certainly, excursions beyond the bounds of topography into wholly imaginative compositions are to be encouraged, for by such enterprise the student is asserting his real independence. Moreover, he is learning to look at Nature for inspiration as well as for assistance, not only in the choice of subject but in the manner in which *he* wants to describe it.

This revelation of a personal view-point of the way in which Nature reveals herself to the painter can be seen by analysing the methods and examining the intentions of the best of the contemporary water-colourists, as well as those of a past generation. Here will be found a variety of expression by which each painter through his paintings can be shown to have learned to *see* for *himself* and to believe in *what he has seen*.

## THE ROUGH

When once you have decided on your chosen subject which you can clearly *see* (and this is so important that I will repeat it) in the terms of a water-colour technique and in *no other medium*, the problem of a good composition should be uppermost in your mind, because it will stand or fall by *how* you arrange the design of your picture. And this is where I may be old-fashioned enough to insist, or anyhow to advise strongly, on your doing a rough or a "try out", if only to confirm your decision that it will make a good subject. So often this preliminary sketch will reveal some unsuspected snag—it may be a matter of too much foreground or a favoured form that has found its way into the centre of your picture—an awkward shape here, a crowded corner or empty area there. All these potential dangers can be checked up and corrected, and once you are satisfied that a good composition has now been obtained, you can press on with your painting with a clear conscience, which will enable you to concentrate solely on the technical painting problems—and they, believe me, will absorb your undivided attention.

These "try outs", moreover, are invaluable for future reference. I have found a number of my own which I am using in this book and which I hope will show their value and uses. Many indeed have remained in the state you see them; others have been used with a certain measure of success in finished water-colours, but none of them has been wasted effort.

RGE ON THE SEINE                    (*In the collection of Sir William Cash*)

TOP—*Winter trees under strong prevailing wind (From the left)*
*Pencil and wash drawing (Payne's grey)*

BOTTOM—*Spring trees under gentle breeze*
*Pencil and wash drawing (Payne's grey)*

# CHAPTER NINE

# Tinted Drawing and Gouache

A WORD or two should be said on the tinted drawing as an alternative to pure water-colour. This can be either a combination of pen and colour or pencil, or chalk with colour. It is of the latter that I can speak with more authority, as I have done little with pen and wash. This is not to say that I have anything against this medium, indeed, in the hand of an expert the mixture of Indian ink and colour can produce pictures of great charm and robustness. It just happens that I find a greater sympathy or affinity between the chalk or pencil line and the subsequent tints than that produced by a steel nib and the rather mechanical evenness of the black ink.

In either technique the colour does no more than support or enhance the general effect. For both processes can either show off or *show up* the artist as a draughtsman. If his drawing is weak, the colour washes do little to flatter the uncertainty of line, but generally draw attention to their meretricious notation.

Given, then, a good sensitive drawing, why—it might be asked—gild the lily? Why add colour? For it is certain that the practice of tinting an etching or a wood engraving is considered unthinkable to the purist in these mediums, who rightly contends that both results need no colour embellishment. But then by each of these methods a richer tone and far more detail may be obtained than is possible or desirable in a drawing, and having executed a number of tinted drawings I can vouchsafe for their

FANTASIA

*(In the collection of Paul Sherwood,*

appeal and justification of the means to this end. If the drawing is crisp in accent, the colour washes do nothing to detract from the sparkle of the touch, but as I have said, show it off to better advantage—or in a better light! Only very transparent washes of pure colour must be floated on, otherwise the tone of the pencil or chalk when overlaid with a mixture of two or more colours will produce a heavy and opaque effect. Indeed, precision of drawing and lightness of handling with the brush are essential if by a combination the two processes are to harmonise with each other. To preserve the maximum clarity of the drawing, this must be fixed before floating on the washes, otherwise the lead or carbon will smudge and lower the tone of the colour scheme.

Very few colours are necessary—nearly all the required shades can be produced with three, blue, yellow and red—as no exact matching of Nature's tints is required.

In subject-matter intimate views are preferable to open land-scapes where skies and other climatic effects need a fuller range of colours.

## GOUACHE

If the technique of pure water-colour proves too difficult, there is always gouache, the name given to a popular medium whereby the pigments can be laid on as in oil painting, but diluted with water instead of turpentine. Being an opaque medium, it is far easier to manage, as the painting is built up in a succession of creamy washes from dark to light. The colours, which are made up in tubes, can be obtained from any artist colourman and are not expensive. A wide range of colours is available—but the fewer the better!

For gouache I advise a special palette. It is fashioned like an enamel cake-tin with six circular slots for mixing your colours. Oil brushes can be used for this medium. Indeed, the approach in handling is similar to oils, as a plastic texture should be aimed at, and your finished painting can be the result of several sittings since the technique offers continual opportunities for repainting.

It must be remembered that all gouache colours dry con-siderably lighter and when they dry have a "matt" finish.

Another warning is due here—if the cap on the tube is not replaced and screwed in firmly, the colour in the tube will quickly dry quite solid.

THE LOG CABIN, WALBERSWICK        *(In the collection of J. F. Horrabin, Esq*

LE LAVANDOU.

CHAPTER TEN

# *Water-colour Sketching Abroad*

S O many of us these days take the opportunity of going
abroad for our holidays that we should also seize the
opportunity (and our sketch-books) to pursue our painting
wherever we elect to go. Sketch-books (in the plural) because it
will come as a delightful surprise to find that almost anything
seen in a foreign country takes on a pictorial significance or "new
look" which cries out to be recorded. The most everyday scenes,
indoor and outdoor, which in our own country, because of their
familiarity, pass unnoticed, now quicken our attention and lend
a sense of urgency to our pencil and brush. It is for that reason
that more than one sketch-book is strongly recommended, and

*Capture authentic reference when you can. Remember—the strongest memory is weaker than the lightest pencil*

more than one size, for it is obvious that the book which can be carried in the pocket and which can be produced at a moment's notice is indispensable for a full recording of all the items of interest which fall within the range of the discerning eye.

A small paint box, three brushes, a container for water and (at least) a dozen pencils, because it is maddening to find that you have only one stub left, and lastly I do advise a light, folding stool because there are times and places where your subject necessitates working in comfort, and this cannot be the case when you are juggling with both hands occupied while still remaining erect!

Whether you travel by train and boat or by plane you will find at every stage of your journey plenty of opportunities to "bag" some authentic reference which memory can never be depended upon to recall with exactness. And the following illustrations will, I hope, give point to this assertion.

Fresh subject-matter for landscape paintings, such as those I have given examples of, will add fresh zest to our work and, if truth be told, present fresh problems to overcome, for climatic conditions will probably prompt a new range of colours, and the varied conditions of situation often demand a speedier and more adventuresome approach than has been found needful when painting on our home ground. In short, our technique gets a good shaking up, and that is an excellent antidote to a conventional and sometimes lethargic way of painting.

And wherever our holiday has been spent, we shall be able to bring back first-hand mementoes of new places seen, new effects noted, and a recorded widening of our artistic vision which I have found opens our eyes afresh to depict on our return the familiar scene as if witnessed by a visitor from abroad! Yes, there is much to be said for sketching in a foreign country—try it and see!

*Pages from the author's sketchbook while in Nice. RAPID pencil sketches made on the road, in cafés, on the front, on station platforms, wherever and whenever the opportunity offered*

*It is surprising how few lines you need to get an impression. And if you've lost your pencil, use your pen!*

OPPOSITE

TOP—The Literal Approach (*South of France*)
*The subject is "down to earth" and painted with realistic truth and vigour as a topographic record of the locality*

BOTTOM—The Personal Approach (*South of France*)
*In this case a tinted drawing is more suitable to the distinctive nature of this tree composition, with its oriental flavour*

*An example of direct painting on the spot wl*

*...ledge of perspective is essential to the success of a composition in depth*

CHAPTER ELEVEN

# *Perspective*

PERSPECTIVE, when once the few simple rules have been explained and understood, will be found to assist the student in all problems where solidity and recession are required. To render relative distances between solid forms, whether they occur in a landscape or an interior subject, can make all the difference between *going in* to a picture or merely *passing across* it. And as one of the most important aims in all picture making is to invite the eye of the beholder to follow the directions of the painter, only by means of perspective can the optical illusion of depth be achieved.

Stripped then of its higher mathematical problems, from which the truly artistic personality naturally shrinks, perspective can be demonstrated by the simple process of using your eyes and believing in what you see and then training the hand to follow their direction.

Thus we all know that the road we are looking along as it goes away from us *appears* to narrow, because our eyes tell us so. We also know that a person walking down this road away from us *appears* to get smaller as the distance grows between us and

OPPOSITE

TOP—*A detailed subject which requires a careful drawing, over which discreet colour washes are introduced to animate the scene. A view of the harbour at St-Tropez*

BOTTOM—*The wayside sketch, which depends for its success on laying in the foreground trees at full strength to render depth and heighten the effect of strong sunshine, characteristic of the Côte d'Azur*

*No perspective. Eye travels across*

*In perspective. Eye travels in*

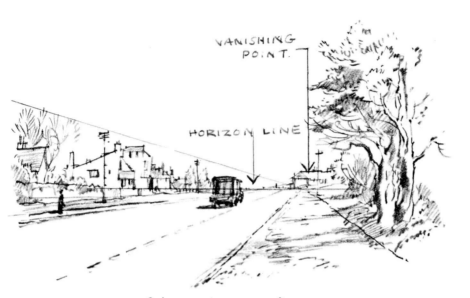

*Only perspective can convey distance*

him. He loses height at the same rate as the width of the road is *seen* to diminish. If telegraph poles (or trees of the same height) stand at regular intervals along this road, they too will be *seen* to shrink in height. And if the road is visible in its entire length (or as far as the eye can see) the sides of the road will *appear* to meet at what we call a vanishing point on the horizon line, i.e. where earth and sky meet.

That is the first and most important fundamental fact, and it is self evident.

What is not so easy to accept, until you have demonstrated it for yourself, is that this horizon line always remains at your own *eye level*. Stand, sit or lie on the ground and watch how the horizon *goes down* with you.

Another fact which has to be pointed out is that parallel lines going to the horizon, which are *above* your eye level (roofs, telegraph lines, etc.) appear to go *down* while those that are *below* your eye, appear to go *up*. And for this reason—that there is only *one* horizon line, and while there can be *more than one*

75

*Looking up from the road gives an unusual sense of perspective. And the introduction of a figure conveys the distance of the house under construction from the rocky foreground*

vanishing point, they must all finish up *somewhere* along this line.

The accompanying diagrams, I hope, will show something of how perspective works. Further and more detailed information I have already given in my book *What Shall We Draw?*

# CHAPTER TWELVE

## *Postscript*

I HOPE in my natural desire to help that I have not posted your suggested route with too many warning signs, which I know can take the edge off your appetite for the pictorial journey. For unlike the road you motor along with its timely warnings of "Steep hill", "Double bend", "Road narrows", etc., all of which are necessary for your safe conduct, the broad highway of water-colour painting should encourage the determination to *arrive* at all costs and even at the risk of repeated accidents! For, after all, there is no loss of life incurred, and the only charge, if charge there is, will be of "careless painting" or "slipshod drawing"; and these two indictments have, I hope, been proved to be real offences in the highway code of water-colour painting! Certain it is that *safety first*, if applied too strictly to this technique, will lead you nowhere.

Finally, without detracting, I hope, from the serious intention of this little work, may I relate an experience (many years ago I am glad to say) when I was newly elected to the Royal Institute of Painters in Water-colours, and showing proudly some of my latest work to a painter for whom I had the greatest admiration and respect. He looked at them in significant silence and then delivered his judgement in two short words—"Very clever". For the record, he didn't say "very" but used a far more telling expletive, now in common use, which made me, as we say "furiously to think". Yes, I thought of that axiom, mentioned

77

in the body of this book, "The danger of admiring the polish and forgetting the table underneath"! You won't forget that, will you? It is so easy when you first take up this fascinating, flattering, fluent, albeit fruitful, medium of water-colour painting.